LIFE LESSONS

LIFE LESSONS

125 Prayers and Meditations

JULIA CAMERON

A TarcherPerigee Book

tarcherperigee

An imprint of Penguin Random House LLC
375 Hudson Street
New York, New York 10014

Most TarcherPerigee books are available at special quantity discounts
for bulk purchase for sales promotions, premiums, fund-raising,
and educational needs. Special books or book excerpts also can
be created to fit specific needs. For details, write: SpecialMarkets@
penguinrandomhouse.com.

LIBRARY OF CONGRESS CATALOGING-IN-PUBLICATION DATA
Names: Cameron, Julia, author.
Title: Life lessons: 125 prayers and meditations / Julia Cameron.
Description: New York: TarcherPerigee, 2017.
Identifiers: LCCN 2017003902 (print) | LCCN 2017012995 (ebook)
| ISBN 9781524704094 | ISBN 9780143130499
Subjects: LCSH: Spiritual life. | Prayers. | Meditations.
Classification: LCC BL624 (ebook) | LCC BL624 .C33165 2017
(print) | DDC 242/.8—dc23
LC record available at https://lccn.loc.gov/2017003902

Printed in the United States of America
10 9 8 7 6 5 4 3 2 1

Book design by Elke Sigal

INTRODUCTION

All too often we yearn for a more spiritual life but tell ourselves it's too difficult. We believe that God is hard to reach and so, discouraged before we begin, we do not even try. The truth is that God is easy for us to reach. The smallest prayer is heard and answered. The simplest overture meets with a loving response.

The tiny book you hold in your hands is a book of simple prayers and meditations—or, if you prefer, a book of simple overtures to God. Each one offers a starting place. Taken collectively, they offer an approach to God that is powerful as well as simple. These prayers are not a one-way street.

They not only allow us to reach out to God, they also allow God to reach out to us.

I have called this little book *Life Lessons* because each entry is a corrective to our commonly held ideas about the divine. Like the postures assumed in hatha yoga, they stretch us gently. As we assume the positions indicated, each entry becomes a lesson. We learn more of God—and of ourselves.

A NOTE FROM THE AUTHOR

In this book you will find that God speaks to you as both "I" and "We." This is because we are sometimes guided by a singular force, and sometimes by a ministry of angels.

1.

Little one, why are you anxious? Why do you worry and fret? I am with you always and I intend you great good. Still your frantic imaginings. Feel my calm. There is no need for panic. You are led carefully and well. There is always a choice: fear or faith. With faith comes the certainty that my world is unfolding exactly as it should. Trust in me. Trust in God—*good, orderly direction*. Everything is in divine order. There is a place for you, safe and protected. Feel my security. I prosper you. You are my child.

2.

Little one, you turn a blind eye to the beauties of my world.

I say to you, "Open your eyes and with your eyes your heart." Dare to love. Dare to appreciate the loveliness all around you. On a snowy night feel my peace and tranquillity. Snowbound, let me be your companion. Feel my calm. I am peaceful and so, too, can you be. Rest your heart in my quietude. Dismantle your fears and trust that all is well.

3.

Dear one, bring me your troubles. I take great joy

in untangling your complicated life. You are overwhelmed but I am not. Your many problems are child's play to me. You have a shadowed heart, but I bring light to it. I illuminate your difficulties. I give you a lantern heart. Ask me for guidance and I will lead you one step at a time. Your path becomes broad and clear. I bring you clarity and grace.

4.

Little one, you have lost a beloved. Your heart is numb, stricken with grief. You feel empty as if your loss has scraped bare the chambers of your heart. Listen to what I tell you now: death is a portal. Your beloved lives on. What you see as an ending is really a beginning. Your loved one feels joy, not sorrow; expansion and freedom as the transition to being "home" brings happiness and peace. Celebrate your beloved's life. Do not mourn what is past. Go forward listening for the subtle signs that life lives on. Your loved one loves you still. Offer prayers of gratitude for all you shared. Your bond continues as you open your heart.

5.

Hurried one, you pray for guidance but then rush on, missing my reply. You tell yourself I ignore you when it is you who ignores my answer. Hear me now: slow down, temper your frantic pace. Velocity is not your friend. Breathe deeply. Open your heart. Inhale the guidance that I would give to you. Focus on the precise moment we are in. Count it as a blessing. My guidance comes to you softly, without haste. Listen.

6.

Little one, you strain for a solution. You push the river seeking an instant answer. You are without patience, without faith. I say to you, "Relax. Let go and let God." My answers are perfect and they come to you with skilled timing. So rest. Do not force events to yield to your will. Trust my timing and my benevolence. I wish you well.

7.

Little one, you feel alone and abandoned.

This is false thinking. You are never alone, never abandoned. We are always at your side, guarding and protecting you. Ask us for help and know that help comes to you. As you slow your pace, you feel our presence. Trust us completely.

8.

Frustrated one, you would force people and situations to do your bidding. Angered, they rebel. You do not get your way. Aggravated, you push still harder. To no avail. So now, pause in your striving. Allow me to advise you: "Easy does it." This is no mere bromide. It doesn't simply mean "slow down." "Easy does it" means "easy accomplishes it." Experiment with this advice. You will find its wisdom.

9.

Stymied one, no one does as you wish! If only

people would follow your lead, all would be well, you believe. But people do as they choose. You find yourself irritated. What is the solution? Put simply, it boils down to a slogan, "Live and let live." Release others to their own agendas and put the focus on yourself: "Live." Follow your heart. Ask what brings it joy. As you follow your bliss, your aggravation with others diminishes. You will know a new freedom and a new happiness. As you "live" you will "let live." Harmony is the result.

10.

Impatient one, you are stern with your animal friends. Instead, take your cue from them. They love you patiently. They are forgiving of your harsh moods. Learn from them. Teach them through love. Praise them. Say to them, "Good little one, good little one." You will find that they respond to kindness. Treat them with love and feel their love come back to you.

11.

Little one, nurture the plants that are in your care.

Play gentle music. Speak to them with love. All living things respond to tenderness. Use discernment in their care. Your intuition will tell you when they are thirsty. Offer them enough water but not too much. Give them nutrients, again, in moderation. Praise their beauty. Appreciate their green life. Take care to give them ample room for growth. Love their verdant spirits. They will flourish in response.

12.

Noisy one, learn to appreciate silence. Learn

to lead your life without a voice-over. The news
of the day is frequently harsh. You hear of
catastrophe, not kindness. Your spirit flags. The
future looms dark. Stop your dire imaginings.
Listen, instead, for the still, small voice that comes
to you with quietude. Mine is a voice of peace,
calm, and optimism. It brings you much good if
you open your heart to receive it. Your heart has
ears that listen acutely. Silence speaks to them.
Listen now and feel your mood gently lifting.

13.

Little one, be alert to tiny things. Do not demand loud noises or showy events. The moon rises softly, blessing the evening air. Stars appear, twinkling on the horizon. As twilight slips into night, a hush comes to the world. Light a candle, burn a stick of incense celebrating the passing of the day. Ask for guidance and feel its gentle hand. You are well and carefully led.

14.

Gentle one, how you please the forces of good.

We are attuned to your whispers. We remind you that all prayers are answered, however small. You speak to us gently and we respond. We hear your soft voice. Your requests come to us on waves of grace. Speaking quietly, you capture our attention. We bring you blessings. Our good will is palpable. Open your heart.

15.

Quiet one, sometimes you criticize your nature. You believe you should be louder to attract our attention. Stop your criticism. You are fine exactly as you are. We have ears for your gentle voice. Your prayers are heard. We listen carefully. Do not strain yourself to become something you are not. In the choir of earthly voices, you bring harmony. Yours is a true note.

16.

Little one, focus on the present. In the exact now you can find peace and harmony. Do not regret the past. Do not dread the future. We are with you always and in each moment you can find our grace. Bless us with your alert attention.

17.

Little one, be willing to be a beginner. Do not demand perfection of your efforts. You are our creation. You are intended to practice creativity yourself. All of your attempts please us. We find grace in your aspirations. Extend to yourself acceptance. Encourage yourself as we encourage you. You are perfect in your imperfection.

18.

Little one, do not judge yourself harshly. Learn to see yourself with kind eyes. Measure yourself not by what you want to do but by how far you've come. Give yourself credit for every tiny step. Praise yourself. Be gentle. Remember that gentleness brings you more success than rigor does. Be tender as a mother bird.

19.

Tired one, allow yourself to rest. Do not push yourself onward, ignoring fatigue. Your body is the beloved vehicle that houses your soul. Treat yourself gently. Do not force yourself forward. Remember H. A. L. T. Do not get too _hungry,_ _angry, lonely, or tired_. Fatigue is dangerous. Rest.

20.

Messy one, bring order to your surroundings that you might bring clarity to your thoughts.

Remember that "Cleanliness is next to godliness." It is difficult to think clearly when your environment is in disarray. Cleanliness brings serenity and serenity brings clear thinking. Spend twenty minutes neatening your world. You will be rewarded by breakthroughs.

21.

Little one, pray for knowledge of God's will for you and the power to carry that out.

Ask the creator for wisdom. Pray not for what you want but rather for what God wants. Seek guidance and follow the guidance you receive. Serenity will be your reward.

22.

Restless one, learn to sit quietly. Take the time to meditate.

Even five minutes will bring results. As you seek quiet contact with your creator, a new balance will be yours. Your intuition will be heightened. You will find a wisdom not your own. You will intuitively know how to handle situations that used to baffle you.

23.

Little one, you long for a more spiritual life but tell yourself it is difficult.

Nonsense. The smallest steps will bring results. Simply say "hello" and our conversation can begin. Whisper my name and I will respond. Listen for me and you will hear the still, small voice. Let us start.

24.

Angry one, you feel the cards are stacked against you. Wait. Consider the possibility that all is well. Ask God to give you the long view. Strive to find the silver lining in adversity. It is always there. Your anger is a form of fear. Admit your fear and ask God to remove it. Feel God's reassurance. You are safe. You are protected. All is well.

25.

Doubting one, set aside your skepticism. Have a child's faith in the good. Trust us completely. Do this by small steps. Begin at the beginning. On a starry night pose for yourself the question, "Who then made all of this?" Consider the moon, serene in its course. Surely there must be a God. Take delight in nature: the hawk, the dove, the deer, the raccoon, even the wily coyote. Something took glee in creation.

26.

Lonely one, you are never alone. At all times, in all places, we are at your side. Say a simple prayer and feel the knife edge of your isolation slip away. Ask us, "Please be with me" and know that we are there. There are forces for good always ready to accompany you. Remember H.A.L.T. and know that the "L" of loneliness is a signal that you should ask for help. Reach out to us and to your fellows. A phone call can be a lifeline. Humble yourself and place a call.

27.

Little one, learn to breathe.
Inhale, saying, "I breathe God in." Exhale, saying, "I breathe me out." Every breath you take creates a bridge to your creator. Every breath you take focuses you in the now. As you breathe in, feel the calm of God. As you breathe out, feel your anxiety slip away. Every breath is a prayer. Feel yourself growing calmer and more centered. Let yourself pray.

28.

Little one, you can meditate simply by walking. Take a step and feel God. Take another step, and feel God again. Each footfall connects you to the earth. Walk slowly. Walk deliberately. Walking is good. Feel God stir your limbs. Step one. Step two. Step three. Step four . . . God is with you every step.

29.

Sad one, allow your sorrow to slip away. Turn your thoughts to the positive. Focus on the now. Feel your well-being. Take a moment to count your blessings. Joy awaits you as you realize you are safe, protected, guarded, and guided. There is a benevolent "something" that intends you good.

30.

Listener, cock your heart's ears to the still, small voice. Quietly ask for guidance and receive it. Say a simple prayer, "Thy will be done," and feel your spirit align itself with your good. You are led carefully and well. There is no error in your path.

31.

Gentle one, your prayers are always heard. Speak in a whisper and know that we are listening. Your faith is firm. You reach out to us without strain. You have learned to hear the still, small voice and you have learned to speak to us in kind. Softly, you request our attention. Softly, we give it to you. Like the dove, you murmur your longings. It is our pleasure to fulfill them. We salute your grateful heart.

32.

Bewildered one, come to us for guidance. Ask for direction and then listen for our cues. We may speak to you through other people. We may speak to you as the still, small voice, the hunch, the inkling. These things are our messengers. Trust the "knowing" that comes to you through prayer. You may be guided by synchronicity. Be alert for signs and signals. Know that as you ask which path to follow you will be led.

33.

Desperate one, your prayers are pitched with anxiety. You feel a dire sense of emergency. You fear the worst. We hear your cries. We know your panic and despair. Only feel our love for you. Feel our compassion for your plight. Where we are present, there is no emergency, no need for panic or despair. You need not beg us for attention. We give it to you gladly. You are safe in our custody. Calm your frantic heart.

34.

Little one, you are tired and that is hard. You must allow yourself rest. Do not use your will as a goad to further exertions. When you are fatigued, all things are difficult. You lose all sense of perspective. The simplest tasks loom large. Your body houses your soul. It is a temple. Rest restores your spirit and your strength, stamina returns to you. Sleep.

35.

Nervous one, your nerves are frayed. You are agitated and ill at ease. You cannot find calm or comfort. Turn to us. Allow us to soothe your psyche. We bring you the assurance that all is well. Divine order prevails. You are safe and protected. We guard and guide you that no harm comes your way. Relax. Breathe deeply. Inhale God. Exhale anxiety. Let every breath become a prayer.

36.

Little one, your friendships are far flung yet they are steady. Your heart is loyal. Your heart is generous. Across great distances your heart holds fast. You have the capacity for deep love. Once you commit, you are steadfast. You love as God loves with stamina and grace. Count your perseverance as a great blessing. We take pride in your steady, loyal heart.

37.

Little one, your love of beauty serves you. As you love the world, you love me. I created this earth that it may fill you with delight. Sunset, moonrise, evening, and then night. Each daily phase brings you joy. The hummingbird, the cardinal, the hawk, each creature has its own delightful nature. As you appreciate the snowfall, quiet comes to your heart. Loving creation, you draw close to the Great Creator.

38.

Little one, snowfall quiets the earth. Each flake lands softly to create a blanket of white. Fir trees wear silver coverlets. Birds take shelter. Jackrabbits leave their prints. All the world seems blessed. Your heart grows still. Calm comes to your restless nature. "Thy will be done," you pray.

39.

Little one, gray gives way to green. The trees are budding. Forsythia burst forth in a golden froth. Spring is here. Robins light on the lamppost. Magpies construct their elaborate nests. It's the will of the Creator that chill earth should blossom. Let your heart, too, open in jubilation. The world is new.

40.

Hurried one, slow your frantic pace.

Stop rushing through your days. When you hurry, you ignore my counsel. There is no time for you to listen. As you move through your day, pause when you are agitated or doubtful. Seek my guidance and pay heed to my advice. If you listen for the still, small voice that gives you direction, it is possible for you to always know the next right step. Only ask me for guidance and it is yours.

41.

Place your hands on your knees. Sit up straight and close your eyes. Inhale. Hold your breath. Count to five. Exhale slowly, saying "ahh." God is in your breath. Inhale, saying, "I breathe God in." Exhale, saying, "I breathe me out." Feel conscious contact with your Creator.

42.

Name five things that give you joy. Choose one and focus on it. Say to yourself, "This world is bountiful. This world is beautiful. This world is abundant." Say to yourself, "I am prosperous." Repeat this as a mantra. Conclude by saying, "This world is blessed."

43.

Little one, consider the radiant moon. Begin with its crescent of light scooped from the sky. Celebrate as it matures. The half-moon promises more radiance to come. See the three-quarter moon yearning to be full. Count your blessings by the light of the full lantern moon. This world is enchanted. Say to yourself and to your Creator, "I love you. Thy will be done."

44.

Timid one, do not be afraid to make yourself known.

In all of creation, I recognize your face. Your soft voice is dear to me. I hear your whispered prayers. Speak to me now. Tell me your joys and sorrows. Allow me to comfort you. You are beloved.

45.

Bold one, I admire your daring. As you leap, I am the net ever ready to catch you. Invisible to the naked eye, I am visible to your heart. We are partners, you and I. We are expansive. We are one power fueling all of creation.

46.

Mourning one, you have lost a beloved. At least

that is how it feels to you. In reality, your beloved
lives on. Death is but a portal to a new and
expanded life. Life survives death. You can make
contact with those who have passed beyond.
Take pen in hand. Address a loving note to your
beloved. Listen for a reply. Loving words will
come to you. Your beloved loves you still.

47.

Gentle one, your words are chamomile to the spirit. You address us softly, and softly we reply. We speak to you gently, grateful for your kindness. A loving bond unites us. Rest assured that our words for you are not mere fantasy. Our connection is real and it brings you great comfort. In turn, you bring us great joy.

48.

Cynical one, you rob yourself of our companionship. Your skepticism

brings you no joy. We reach out to you and you

tell yourself our touch is your imagining. We speak

to you and you discount our voice. How can we

convince you we are real? If you will listen and

write down what you hear, you will find our words

give you wise counsel. Our voice is calm and clear.

Let our wisdom teach you to trust us.

49.

Little one, greet us on awakening.

Let your day begin with our contact. Ask us for guidance and heed what you hear. We direct you carefully and well. We assure you that you are safe and protected. We intend you great good. We hold you in loving custody. Acknowledge this as you begin your day. As you ask to be guided step-by-step, our wisdom comes to you. You are never alone, never without our counsel. Simply say "good morning" and let our conversation begin.

50.

Little one, end your day by making contact. Thank us for the hours just passed. Gently examine your day. Were you in alignment with our wishes? At day's end, count your blessings. Allow yourself to feel gratitude for the many small things that have gone well. We guard you as you sleep.

51.

Little one, the trees are lit like bonfires. Winter is coming on. Let your heart take its cues from God's tempo. The air is crisp and you must dress warmly against the cold. Icicles grace the eaves. Enjoy their beauty. Do not fight the chill. Instead, find the season bracing. Appreciate God's timing.

52.

Loud one, do not shout your prayers.

We have ears for the softest whisper. Do not raise your voice to capture our attention. There is no need. We hear your sighs. We hear your whispered prayers. Speak softly and know that you command our attention. Calm your fearful heart that speaks with a strident voice. There, my child. Be gentle. You are heard.

53.

Little one, you fear our contact.

You are afraid that our will for you is harsh and counter to your own wishes. This is not the case. Our will for you is joyous. Your deepest desire is also our will for you. Your will and God's will are not at opposite ends of the table. As you pray, try saying, "Thy will be done." You will find your own will gently tempered. You will come to desire what the divine desires for you. Ask for an understanding of God's will. As you are given the power to carry it out, you will feel an abiding contentment.

54.

Gentle one, it pleases us to watch you move through the world. We see your kindness. We see your tender ways. When you meet with adversity, you ask for grace. You pray for an understanding of God's will for you. You look for the silver lining. Your faith and your optimism serve you. You trust divine order. You are well and carefully led.

55.

Edgy one, your anxiety shadows your days. You face the future with feelings of apprehension. What is called for is a gentle discipline. When your thoughts run to the negative, rein them in. Focus on the moment. Ask yourself, "Am I not okay?" Take yourself in hand. Breathe deeply. Feel your anxiety slip away. Be vigilant concerning your dark moods. Allow a sense of optimism to wash over you.

56.

Depressed one, you move through your days saddled with sorrow. Your moods are dark. No matter what good comes to you, you look for the woeful side. Seeking darkness, you find it. Stop. Stop your painful imaginings. Ask us to help you. We can lighten your heavy heart. We can guide you to simple actions that lift your esteem. Ask us to love you. We can teach you to love yourself. Self-love cures depression. Let us help you to heal.

57.

Little one, turn your eyes to beauty. See the marvels of my world. Look to the hummingbird that flits lightly through the air. Dip your head to smell the roses. Track the moon in the nighttime sky. The calico cat suns itself on the window ledge. The silken puppy dances with glee. All of these things bring joy to your heart, and joy is the portal to the divine.

58.

Tidy one, your order invites grace.

You have heard the expression, "Cleanliness is next to godliness." This is true. As you order your surroundings, great good comes to you. The divine is meticulous. The world is made of interlocking parts, each one in its place. You are a gear in the universe. Your orderly, graceful placement contributes to the whole.

59.

Kindly one, your gentle soul brings us much joy. We watch as you move through the world, touching all with tenderness. In your every interaction, you bring grace to bear. You are always aware of the divine spark in every individual. You treat all with respect and this pleases us. You are a messenger of our love. We intend you great good.

60.

Lonely one, reach to us for companionship. We

are with you always although you seldom sense
our presence. Know that Spirit touches you. Ask
us to let you feel our touch. When you pray for
guidance, we draw near. We speak to you with a
still, small voice. Listen closely and you will hear
us. Hearing us, know that you are not alone.

61.

Little one, reach out to us that we may guide

you. It is our duty and our joy to give you
direction. Ask us throughout your day what your
next step is to be. Listen closely. We will shepherd
you carefully and well. Do not try to pass your day
without our aid. Ask us always for our help. We
give it to you gladly. At all times, you are guided
and guarded. You are in our safekeeping and we
intend you great good.

62.

Impatient one, you do not trust our timing.

Instead, you rush ahead pursuing your desires. You lack patience. You lack the wisdom to await outcomes. So I say to you, "Try to trust. Surrender your rushed tempo." Allow events to unfold at their natural pace. Do not hurry ahead. Relax your urgency. Remember, "Easy does it."

63.

Fearful one, you face your day with apprehension. You anticipate

the worst. You do not enjoy the situations you are in. Instead you look to the future with dread, frightened of what is to come. Your ego yearns for control. Stop your anxiety. Your soul is safe and protected. Bring yourself back to the current moment. Are you not all right? In the present moment, you are always cared for. In the future, you will be cared for as well. This I promise you. You are safe in my custody. Release your fears. Breathe in God. Breathe out anxiety. All is well.

64.

Little one, you feel yourself small as the events in your life loom large. Listen to what I say. You are large enough to face any catastrophe. We gift you with size enough to handle each event. You are not too small. Rather you are a part of us and we are very big. Ask us for strength and know that we answer you. Feel yourself grow in faith. Faith is all that is required of you. Faith makes you large.

65.

Frightened one, come to us with your fears.

Tell us what troubles you. Lay your anxiety at our feet. Practice candor by revealing your woes. Unburden your heart, trusting us to listen. We have ears for all parts of you. No fear is too large or too small. Let us reassure you. You are safe and protected. You are ours.

66.

Little one, allow yourself to love my world. I made this world for your delight. It is filled with beauty. Allow yourself to relish its loveliness. Hollyhocks stand sentinel in my gardens. Delphiniums stand tall as well, sporting a vibrant blue, cobalt like the evening sky. Shy violets grow at the feet of mighty oaks. Willow trees swish with the wind. The graceful garter snake slides into the tall grasses. The llama blinks a gentle eye. The sporty zebra wears a dashing coat. The gazelle runs swiftly over the plains. All these wonders and many more are yours.

67.

Little one, you pray for guidance and then you ignore it as it comes. You tell yourself our guidance is just your imagination. This is not the case. When you ask for our help, we give it to you, but our wisdom is subtle and so you discount it. Learn to listen to the still, small voice. Pay attention to synchronicity. Our guidance comes to you in many forms. Be alert for signs and signals. Be alert for our presence. We come to you when you ask.

68.

Little one, let yourself believe. As you ask us to come to you, we do. Feel our presence. We are real. When you reach to us, we reach back. When you speak to us, we answer. There are higher forces that intend you good. This is a fact. Accept us as reality. Come to us and many blessings come back to you.

69.

Faithful one, you bring us great joy. As you practice optimism, you draw close to us. As you come near, we bring you blessings. It gives us joy to bless you. We are an expansive energy and as you receive our gifts, we feel gifted in return. Your acceptance of our presence fills us with happiness. We are united.

70.

Silent one, why are you afraid to speak? Why do

you fear our contact? We intend you nothing but good. Reach out to us and feel our loving embrace. Utter a prayer, speaking softly. Say to us, "Thy will be done," and feel the peace of our kind intentions. We are always with you, always listening for your voice. Speak to us now and feel our connection. Do not fear. We bring you joy.

71.

Joyful one, we touch your heart. As you count your blessings, they multiply. As you list your gratitudes, we greet your grateful heart. Reaching to us, you are filled with grace. It is our gift to you. We appreciate your openness to spiritual realms.

72.

Little one, ask us to prosper you. Know that your bottom line is spiritual not fiscal. Ask us for security and we will give it to you. Ask and you will feel our abundance. All riches are first spiritual. We contain wealth beyond your imagining. You are prospered as you believe.

73.

Little one, come to us for abundance. As you ask to

be prospered, we prosper you. As you expect

plenty, we prove ourselves plentiful. Our coffers

are full to overflowing. Accept our riches. We are

abundant and so, too, are you.

74.

Loving one, you are generous of spirit and your generosity brings us joy. As you seek to cherish all you encounter, we bring you blessings that you have earned. Each time you reach out to others, we reach out to you. You draw on our unlimited resources. We bless you as a kindred spirit. Accept our love.

75.

Little one, let us give
you direction that you
may find yourself well
and carefully guided.

Take pen in hand. Pose a question or issue on
which you need guidance. Ask us to shepherd
you and then listen for our response. Write out
the words that you "hear." You will find we are
wise, clear, and kind. Seek our guidance daily
and you will come to trust us. Try it now.

76.

Little one, give freely of what you have. Extend yourself

to others less fortunate. Ask us for grace that you

may feel yourself replenished. It is a spiritual law

that as you give you will be given to. We are rich

beyond your imagining. We prosper you that you

may prosper others in turn.

77.

Hopeless one, how can we coax you to optimism? How can we give you faith? We'll begin at the beginning with the natural world. Rise early one day and greet the rising sun. See it illuminate the world. Next, at midday, appreciate its even light. Watch for twilight and then nightfall. The sun has spent its course. It does so daily, and you can find in its path a lantern for your own. Live each day to the fullest. Look neither to the future nor to the past. Each day is a new beginning. Cherish it.

78.

Little one, we want you to trust yourself. We want you to trust your guidance. As you turn to us, we hold a light to your path. The road before you is broad and gentle. Each step is clear. You can depend on us to give you careful guidance. You are well led as you ask us the course to take. Do not doubt the direction in which we lead you. Trust us and trust yourself.

79.

Procrastinator, you know the next step but you postpone. You hang back, fearful of commitment. Turn to us for the willingness to go forward. Ask us for strength and energy. We have unlimited power. We gladly offer you help. As you go forward you will sense our grace. Our resources are yours to use.

80.

Bewildered one, left to your own devices you do not know which path to choose. Turn to us for guidance. We give you the gift of direction. We promise you a path that is broad and bright.

Ask us which step to take. We will lead you carefully and well. As you pray, intuition will come to you. No longer baffled, you will step forward.

81.

Sloppy one, your messiness is a detriment.

When your surroundings are untidy, your thinking
is unclear. Take time to neaten your environment.
Ask us for clarity and energy. We will give you
the gift of discernment. As you work to straighten
your domain, we will give you breakthroughs.
Serene surroundings lead to serene thoughts.
Tidiness yields godliness. Feel our grace.

82.

Little one, you are
confused. You do not
know which path to
take. Turn to us for guidance. Ask to be led.
As you seek our direction, you enable us to steer
you. Once again, take pen in hand and write out
our advice. Our guidance is wise and clear. The
still, small voice speaks to you quietly, but you can
hear it. Listen and you will be led.

83.

Shy one, you hesitate to make yourself known.

You put others forward believing them to be more worthy. This is an error. You are more than worthy of our attention. Step forward. Claim your place in the sun. You are deserving of our notice. Despite your trepidation, we see you and know you. You are blessed and cherished.

84.

Little one, you second guess yourself. You ask for guidance, receive it, and then discount it. When you ask for our help, we readily give it to you. There is ease, grace, and wisdom in our communication. The fact that our guidance comes easily is no reason to dismiss it. Do not equate the spiritual life with difficulty. We come to you with ease. Accept our direction. Do not doubt that we are real.

85.

Little one, we come to you in a variety of ways.

Sometimes we speak directly as the still, small voice. At other times, we speak to you through people. Still other times, we come to you as a hunch or intuition. And sometimes, we signal to you through synchronicity. When you ask to be guided, be alert to the many ways our guidance may appear. Know that you are never alone, never unshepherded. The universe is responsive to your needs. Be alert. No prayer goes unanswered.

86.

Little one, learn to ask for help in all aspects of your life. Do not set aside some as taboo. Romance and finance are the two areas most often left unprayed about. Yet these are the two topics with which we often need the most help. Experiment now. Write a letter to the universe stating your needs, hopes, and desires. Trust that it is safe to be candid.

87.

Little one, speak to us freely. Trust that as you pray, we listen.

Share with us your secret heart. We have ears for every part of you. There is nothing foreign to us. We have compassion and empathy for you. Trust us to treat your confessions gently. You cannot shock us. We have seen and heard the whole of human experience. We welcome your candor and bless you in response.

88.

Little one, we can help you to integrate your experiences. You may feel torn asunder, pulled in opposing directions by your life. We have an overview. We see how the many puzzle pieces fit together. Share with us the contradictory elements that leave you baffled. We will gift you with healing insights that mend your scattered life.

89.

Little one, your need is exercise. Your body is the beloved vehicle that houses your soul. Even the smallest amount of physical exertion does you well. Put on some walking shoes and set out for twenty minutes. As you walk, insights will come to you. Remember the words of St. Augustine: *Solvitur ambulando*—"It is solved by walking."

90.

Little one, there is time enough. Do not lag behind or rush forward. Instead, attune your cadence to ours. We move at a moderate pace. Divine timing is always perfect, neither too fast nor too slow. Look to the seasons. They unfold perfectly and so, too, can you. When you feel anxiety at your life's pacing, remind yourself to pray. Ask to be guided. Ask for the wisdom to accept divine order. Tell yourself gently, "All is well."

91.

Little one, ask for creativity. Remember that all ideas are divine in origin. The Great Creator thinks through us. We are the conduits through which the Creator's inventiveness enters the world. Ask to be an open channel. Ask to be an instrument in God's hands.

92.

Little one, open your heart to love. Ask to be supplied with love. There is one energy flowing through all creation. That energy is love. Know that you are beloved and that you are intended to love in return. Mystics tell us that God is love. Have faith in their message. Great souls all declare the same truth.

93.

Little one, meditate on one thought: God is love. As you focus on this fact, feel a great calm coming to your consciousness. Listen for the still, small voice that declares, "Be still and know that I am God." Quiet your mind, resting in the certitude that God is all and all is love. Breathe deeply knowing that all is well, all is good, and all is God.

94.

Little one, rest in our embrace. Quit all striving. Know that

all is well. The world is in divine order. There is a

place for you, cherished and serene. Do not feel

you must earn our love. We love you freely.

We have loved you since the beginning of time.

We will continue to love you through eternity.

Rest secure in our love for you. All is well.

95.

Sleepy one, let yourself
rest. Do not push forward ignoring your
fatigue. Remember H.A.L.T.: do not get too
hungry, angry, lonely, or tired. Fatigue is the
enemy of well-being. Fatigue breeds fear and a
devastating sense of impending doom. Therefore,
rest when you are tired. Allow sleep to mend the
raveled seams of care. Rest, knowing that when
you wake the world will seem a better place.

96.

Little one, take your life one day at a time. Do not

linger in the past or rush ahead into the future.
Take your cue from nature. Time is divided by
night into days. Each day is a single scoop of
experience. Measure your life likewise. Each day
contains "enough." Be gentle with yourself.
Learn the wisdom of God's timing.

97.

Little one, learn to take first things first. Order your day

according to our guidance. Put first those things
we indicate. As you follow our direction, you
will experience well-being. The orderly timing
of events brings peace to your psyche. Say to
yourself, "Thy will be done," and then follow your
intuition. Remember that G.O.D. stands for
"good, orderly direction."

98.

Little one, it is God's will for us to be creative.

Ask us to give you inspiration. You will be led carefully and well. When you undertake a creative project, listen for the still, small voice. Ask us for help. We will lead you one step at a time.

99.

Little one, you are confused. You do not know which path to take. Ask us for a hunch or intuition. We will guide you. Listen for our voice. Pray for knowledge of our will for you and the power to carry it out. Pray, saying, "Thy will be done." As you ask for guidance, we will give you a sense of direction. We will help you to know the next right step. We are always with you and our guidance is always available. Only ask for help and then listen. You are safe and protected in our custody. We shelter you. We lead you with care. We guide you accurately. Be alert for our promptings. Trust our lead.

100.

Little one, pray always.

Turn your thoughts to us and ask us for guidance.
Do not try to go through your day alone. Instead,
seek our companionship. Ask us to guard and
guide you. Seek conscious contact. We are
always ready to greet you. Say to us, "Thy will be
done," and we will give you direction. No prayer,
however small, goes unanswered. Only listen.

101.

Little one, your soundtrack lacks serenity.

Be alert. Focus on the noise level in your environment. Tune in peace and well-being. Tune out harsh decibels. Be merciful. Even the plants you nurture thrive on soothing melodies. They prefer Mozart to hard rock. They prefer ragas to jazz. Allow yourself to bathe in a sonic soup that is gentle and enriching. Remember that we speak of having a "sound body." Take that expression literally. It is a directive. Make sound choices in sound.

102.

Little one, trust your intuition. Ask for guidance and then pay close attention to the hunches that emerge. The still, small voice speaks to you often as intuition. It is the "funny feeling" that leads you down one path and not another. It is the subtle sense of "knowing" the next right action. You will intuitively know the answer to what used to baffle you. As you practice it, your intuition gradually becomes a working part of the mind. You will come to rely on it.

103.

Little one, learn to discern the voices you hear within. Our voice is always calm; our advice is wise and simple. Learn to discard the voices that are strident. Harsh, hurried, and pushy advice does not come from us. Take the time to listen carefully. Which voice is speaking?

104.

Little one, learn to rely

on us. It is strength, not weakness, to ask for our help. We are an unlimited resource. Turning to us, you tap an unlimited supply. There is no problem too harsh or complex for us. Draw on us freely. It is our pleasure to come to your aid.

105.

Puzzled one, turn to us for answers. Ask us for guidance and then listen closely. We bless you with intuition. From deep within you, an answer will emerge. Trust your knowing. The still, small voice leads you carefully and well. In our custody, you are guarded and guided. Pray for an end to your confusion. Clarity will come.

106.

Little one, you are wiser than you know. As you pray for guidance, you are indeed guided. As you ask for wisdom, you are made wise. Turn to us now. Rely on our strength. Ask for intuition and you will be given a hunch about which path to take. By depending on us, you become sure-footed. We are that lantern you can see by. Your path is broad and brightly lit.

107.

Little one, eat when you are hungry. Do not ignore your appetite. Remember H.A.L.T. Do not get too *hungry, angry, lonely, or tired*. Hunger breeds depression and a misplaced sense of drama. When you are well fed, you will experience a sense of well-being, and that is the bedrock of faith.

108.

Little one, avoid crazy makers, those individuals who generate storms. Crazy makers create dramas—but seldom where they belong. They break deals and destroy schedules. They expect special treatment. Crazy makers discount your reality and pretend *you're* crazy. Learn to identify the crazy makers in your midst. Give them a wide berth.

109.

Lonely one, we are with you at all times although you seldom sense our presence. We are by your side, closer than your breath. When you need companionship, turn to us. More than any human, we are your friend. When you crave company, come to us with your craving. Allow us to soothe the anxious pangs of loneliness. We are with you now.

110.

Little one, there is a divine plan of goodness for you. We guard and guide you. You are safe in our custody. Regard the natural world. See how every plant and animal is given what they need. Know that you, too, are looked after with a plan of equal care. You are never alone, never abandoned. Higher forces watch over you with infinite love.

111.

Little one, your dreams are known to us. Your secret hopes and desires are in our safekeeping. As you open your heart to us, we are able to keep your dreams safe and protected. As you express your creativity, we welcome it. Never doubt that it is God's will for you to be creative. Creativity is God's nature and your own.

112.

Little one, you worry that you bother me. You are afraid that you pester me, that you get on my nerves. This is not the case. I am always glad to hear from you. I have infinite patience, and our contact fills me with joy. You are never a bother. Instead, you are a delight. I always have ears for you and your troubles, however petty they may seem to you. Know that I cherish you. I am delighted to have you call my name.

113.

Dear one, you fret that you are lost among the multitudes. So many call on me that you doubt your voice can be heard. Stop your worry. You are known to me. Amid the crowd I can always hear your voice. Do not imagine that you are lost or abandoned. I am infinite. My ability to love is without limit. You are dear to me. Amid the throngs of creation, you are particular. I know every hair on your head. I cherish you.

114.

Little one, I find you beautiful. Every muscle and sinew, every hair, even every freckle is dear to me. I am your creator and I made you beautiful. Learn to see yourself through my eyes. Recognize your loveliness and your grace. Do not fret over imagined flaws. You are perfect precisely as you are.

115.

Little one, you are perfect in your imperfection. I accept you exactly as you are. Where you see shortcomings, I see your attempts at more and better. Where you see failure, I see effort exerted that may fall short but was nonetheless tried. You flagellate yourself for flaws. I focus instead on all that you do right. Borrow my eyes. See your perfection.

116.

Little one, take delight in my world. I made it beautiful that it might enchant you. A cardinal flits from a tree. Its scarlet coat is dashing. A golden retriever bounds by its owner's side. Its exuberance is contagious. Spotting it, you feel joy. A piebald horse grazes by the roadside. You sense its contentment as it nibbles sweet clover. The willow tree dances in the wind. The maple tree sports its crimson leaves. All this and more I made for your enjoyment. Love this world, and, loving it, love me.

117.

Little one, count your blessings. Begin at the beginning with your senses. All of them—taste, touch, smell, hearing, sight—bring you joy. You have much to be grateful for: your health, your livelihood, your dwelling, your friendships, your skills. Surely some part of you seems perfect: your eyes, your ears, the hair on your head, your hands, your feet, your breasts. Bless all of you and, as you do, witness your blessings as they multiply.

118.

Lively one, your gaiety brings us joy. We rejoice in your laughter. We celebrate your glee. You are correct that this world is not intended to be a vale of tears. Instead, you find it beautiful and in beauty you find happiness and in happiness you find God. Joy, not suffering, is the portal to the divine. Let your exuberant heart lead you home.

119.

Little one, practice compassion.

Open your soul and extend its loving kindness to those you meet. Refrain from harsh judgments. Instead, extend your empathy to all you encounter. Recognize the divine spark in each and every person. Treat friends and strangers with sympathetic understanding. Ask us for the grace to greet the world with compassion. The world will treat you in kind.

120.

Little one, prosper and flourish.

Draw your abundance from God's unlimited supply. Share your prosperity with others. Receive plenty and extend plenty to those you meet. You are given to generously. Be generous in turn. Know that there is always enough—more than enough—for every soul to thrive. Nurture your companions. Give freely, trusting that you will be given to in return. God rewards a generous heart.

121.

Little one, do not fear lack.

Know that this is an abundant world containing plenty for everyone. Trust divine supply. Draw on God's prosperity. Acknowledge God as your source and realize God's wealth is unlimited. You are a child of God and your inheritance is rich. Count on God to supply your needs and to gift you with "more" as you supply the needs of others.

122.

Little one, learn from your animal companions. Practice having the open heart and unconditional love they show to you. Focus on the here and now, looking neither to the past nor to the future. Celebrate the precise moment you are in as the dog does with its glad tail. Express your appreciation for the present as the cat does with its gentle purr. Your animals have much to teach you. Humble yourself and learn.

123.

Little one, surrender your sense of urgency.

There is no emergency. Trust God: Good, Orderly Direction. Accept the wisdom of your own unfolding. Receive God's timing as your own. Cultivate calm. Do not rush forward, pushing events to unfold with unnatural speed. The universe moves at the precise pace that serves your highest good. Trust divine order to be in your best interests. Relax your tempo.

124.

Little one, open your mind and heart to the plan of service that most benefits you and others. Feel joy as our direction unfolds within you. Undertake actions that empower and embody your guidance. Release others from your agendas, trusting that the perfect people and events will arise to greet them as you follow your own path. Moving forward as you are inwardly guided, ask, always, to be of service. Doing so yields joy for you and for others.

125.

Little one, your perceptions are alert and accurate. In times of doubt, remind yourself that your sensitivity is acute. You know—and notice—what you need to know. You register people and events accurately. Your guidance is subtle and keen. Denial does not block your perceptions. You are shrewd and knowledgeable. Appearances do not deceive you. You sense the truth and respond accurately to reality. You are grounded and safe.

ABOUT THE AUTHOR

Julia Cameron is the author of more than forty books, including such bestselling works on the creative process as *The Artist's Way*, *Walking in This World*, and *Finding Water*. A novelist, playwright, songwriter, and poet, she has multiple credits in theater, film, and television. She divides her time between Manhattan and the high desert of New Mexico.